Time and the Tilting Earth

LOUISIANA STATE UNIVERSITY PRESS ❧ BATON ROUGE

Miller Williams

Time and the Tilting Earth

POEMS

Published by Louisiana State University Press
Copyright © 2008 by Miller Williams
All rights reserved
Manufactured in the United States of America
First printing

DESIGNER: Amanda McDonald Scallan
TYPEFACE: Mrs Eaves
PRINTER AND BINDER: Thomson-Shore, Inc.

Library of Congress Cataloging-in-Publication Data

Williams, Miller.
  Time and the tilting earth : poems / Miller Williams.
    p. cm.
  ISBN 978-0-8071-3352-1 (alk. paper) — ISBN
978-0-8071-3353-8 (pbk. : alk. paper)
  I. Title.
  PS3545.I53352T56 2008
  811'.54—dc22

                    2007047237

Thanks to the editors of ABZ, *Arkansas Literary Forum*, *Arts & Letters*,
Chariton Review, *Concerning Poetry*, *Enskyment*, *Georgia Review*, *Massachusetts
Review*, *Measure*, *New Letters*, *Oxford American*, *Prairie Schooner*, *Press Time*,
Shenandoah, *Southern California Anthology*, *Terminus*, *Totem*, *Vanderbilt
Review*, and *Visions International* in which some of these poems have
appeared.

A very special thanks to Jo McDougall.

for Jordan

Contents

Time and the Tilting Earth

An Unrhymed Sonnet

What is existence? What does it mean to be?
How did existence come to be from nothing?
Is nothing lying still at the core of being?
Why is there life? If life began with God,
did God have a beginning? If God was always,
how did God and always come to be?
If neither began, if they run all the way back,
they run back all the way to what, to when?

If time is a long illusion, what is always?
What hangs itself around the universe?
If this one universe is all there is,
all the more the question wants an answer.

Excuse me. I shouldn't ask these questions here.
Please—just go ahead and cut my hair.

After All These Years of Prayer and Pi R Square

How sweet a confusion that science, that creed of the creature,
that earthly philosophy of numbers in motion,
distrusted so by rabbi, sheik, and preacher
who have clothed its nakedness in flame,
should quietly introduce us to the notion
of something weightless within us wanting a name.

Epithalamium

It would sound good to say that chairs and doors,
cups and buttons, books and ballpoint pens,
will not be what they were before the joining
of these two people who are lovers and friends.
It would sound better to say the change is all
in him and her but if, in the world's fact,
these both are lies and there is little that changes,
still there's a gladness in the ritual act.

Say that these who please each other have chosen
to live their lives together and thereby touch,
to let his door be hers and her door his.
Some may think this isn't very much
to marry for, but others think it is.

How Step by Step We Have Come to Understand

In the sixteenth century Nicholas Copernicus
told us the earth was a ball and, what was worse,
was not the center of the universe.
"Well and so," we wanted to know,
"where does that leave us in the scheme of things?"

Wherever it left us,
we were barely learning to live with it
when three centuries later Charles Darwin
grabbed our attention with the news
that we were cousins to the kangaroos.
"And so," we wanted to know,
"where does that leave us in the scheme of things?"

Wherever it left us,
we were barely learning to live with it
when half a century later Albert Einstein,
making a myth of tomorrow, a myth of place,
told us there only seemed to be time and space.
"So," we wanted to know,
"where does that leave us in the scheme of things?'

Wherever it left us,
we were barely learning to live with it
when thirty years later Werner Heisenberg
told us we were only manifestations
of probability curves and colliding equations.
"So," we wanted to know,
"where does that leave us?"

Wherever it left us,
we were barely learning to live with it
when here came Flannery O'Connor and Hank Williams
to tell us that no one has ever been loved
the way everybody wants to be loved,
and that's hard. That's hard.

A Note from When I Was Here to Anyone Here

April 19. Sunday. Uncommonly warm.
The *Times* details signs of the coming collapse,
tells of a generation of casual killers
making its way past puberty in small towns,
of lakes and rivers all the fish are gone from,
reports the prayers of women with covered faces
who beg for the end of war, the return of their sons,
and gives the financial news with ingenious graphs.

It also invites subscriptions, which we can take
as an act of faith in delay, in possibly not.

If you are there, are here, and you can read this,
mostly we hoped you would be, mostly we do,
and there were some who tried to make that likely,
though not me much, nor many that I knew.

Some Lines to a Dog Who Doesn't See the Difference

I know that you know more than I recognize,
and slowly I have almost learned to read
vocabulary and grammar in your eyes,
but we can never be the same breed.
I have to use my fingers when I feed
and you could never learn to tell me lies.
Believe me a dog, my friend, but then be glad
to lie down to a dream I've never had.

Irony in the Real World

We're warned to be more careful with our seed,
that we're about to be too many to feed,
that all our waste is making the earth a mess,
that horrible times are ahead of us unless
we use our pills and rubbers. This is true,
but what will a generation some day do,
facing the fact that the only ones who heeded
the admonition carried the genes they needed?

Thoughts on an Anniversary
Once More, with Feeling

Well, here we are again, with the same old brain,
or nearly the same—the light's a little dimmer—
still knowing not what we are, just what we do.
But, wait. If in that doing there might be a clue
to something too simple for anyone to explain,
something we try to forget and wish we knew,
call this the celebration of a glimmer.

Once more: a gentle touch, and molecules
line up along the wall of a neural chain
at the links of which a thing called acetylcholine
passes the signal on till it reaches the brain
where it's read as pleasure as opposed to pain.

When such a signal begins in the head, as a thought,
and goes to a muscle, it makes the muscle contract
and leaves as a by-product some lactic acid.
Because it makes it hard for the cells to react,
the acid is read as fatigue. As a matter of fact,

we're all of us laboratories, but you won't think
of all the splitting and bonding taking place
when you're wrestling your dog or washing the car
or rocking a child or watching a liar's face
or leaning into the wind or a slow embrace.

This may be what it means to be what we are—
that something in the doing of what we do
makes matter matter less and truth less true.

The Old Professor Deals with Death and Dying

Talking around the block with no one near
but me, my sometime friend,
I think of events that punctuate our lives
and how, as a kindness deep in the nature of things,
death brings the sentence to an end.

How many of us, though,
when vessels break and minds misconstrue,
will say inside ourselves that we'd rather be dead
except that we're scared to die?
More than a few,
hardly disturbing the bedsheets, have said—
telling not quite the truth, not quite a lie—
"Lord, I don't want to die. I just want to be dead."

They'd leave living behind and go back to what
they were before they were born. Who can recall
a lot of discomfort in that? Like as not,
we're all of us going to no place at all,
a nowhere with nothing to pay, nothing to do,
no one to do it with and no one to care.
What a crock to have to suffer through
a damned initiation to get only there.

Still we stand at the beds of those who leave us
and cherish the seconds. Still our best dramas
depend on the death scenes, which all the religious
tell us are not periods but commas.

Something That Meant to Be a Sonnet
for an Anniversary Evening

I walk around them in silence, those who say
that making ourselves ready for judgment day
is the one reason we're here, and those who insist
that we're no more than water with a twist.
Sometimes they take my arm. I tell them, "Okay,
that makes sense to me," and move away.
Clearly there's something somewhere that I've missed.
Somehow we probably do and don't exist,
but all these finer subtleties fell to the floor
the night you opened the window and closed the door
and smiled in a frozen curve that burned to be kissed.

A Note to the Alien on Earth

Here, in the interest of time, some words to work with,
assuming you're pretending to be a man
or woman and understand English. If this should find you,
know that I'm glad to help any way I can:

A letter beginning "Dear Friend" is not from a friend.
A "free gift" is redundant and not free.
A teenager is sex with skin around it.
The one word used as much as "I" is "me."

People who are politically correct,
which means never offending by what they say,
will lie about other things, too. Be careful with them.
And people insulting other people may

look in the mirror too much or not enough.
What you say is not what anyone hears.
Be wary of one who is always or never sad.
And try to be patient with us. It looks bad,
but we've had only a few hundred thousand years.

The More Things Change

I need time, we've cried, and I need space,
without knowing what it was we wanted.
Now, though, we know. There's something called space-time.
Not seeming to have dimension, it has a texture.
Like the paper these words are lying on,
it folds back on itself, it wrinkles and tears,
and people rolled in their coats sleep on sidewalks.

Space and time are perceptions, known as *local events,*
invented by energy posing as stuff. Still,
two shapes coming together can kill us, like cars,
or start a new life along its way to daylight.

A positron, we've learned, is just an electron
moving backward in what we take as time,
and people preserve other people and put them in boxes.

Matter's been made by the merging of light beams,
though this doesn't matter to people who break into homes
the darkest hour of the night, or to those being born.

He said it was all a play. How did he know
that what we can see and do is a long illusion?

Making up our lines as we go along,
we shout or mumble the last ones and leave the scene,
wondering if the curtain will ever fall,
to leave at the center of nothing a lonely knowledge
that may sit everywhere watching us play our parts,

some of us for a century, some for an hour,
claiming our time on a stage we still want to call
our world, our science, our altars, and our arts,
all seemingly trying to say to us, *This is not all.*

Sitting in a Bar after a Poetry Reading

Today may be as good a day as any
to come to terms with what we know is true.
There may be some who have. There may be many.
None of them can tell us what to do.

You sit at the center of nothing. Squint as you will,
you'll never see your way out of this.
I wouldn't say to shut your mouth. Still,
silence has an eloquence. You miss

the point of what I'm trying to say here.
But that's the point. To put it all together
you have to take it apart. If I appear—
what do I want to say?—as if another

way of going has made its home in my head,
it doesn't matter. Whatever has control
will say whatever serves by being said.
The sum of the parts is greater than the whole

when what we're talking about is literature—
poetry in particular—and how extremely
important it seems to be when it's obscure.
Although to say this seems somewhat unseemly,

it's hard to be understood and make that look easy,
which may be why it's done by very few.
A famous poet today, adroit as you please, he
makes look hard what any drunk can do—

conceal a meaning in sound. But I'm afraid
I've thrown my one chance to make it away.
I wanted to show you how a poem is made,
but you may have understood what I meant to say.

Helping a Lady of Eleven Get Her Lessons

She falls asleep reading on the floor,
letting her head
rest on the back of her dog. I'd put her to bed
but he moves first, and now she's back to the book,
like she needs to know more
than anybody ever knew before.
She tells me with a clearly classroom look
that she's ready to go.

The first thing she wants to know,
holding a picture some anthropologist took,
is any difference between those people and us.

Well, I tell her, the currency, the language—plus,
some of them don't like us and we do.
It comes down to the table. Only a few
whose luck it is to be stuck outside the gate,
smelling the rump roasting, can help but hate
the souls inside and being told to wait
when nobody's drawn a circle around a date.
Some of the people whose people are standing out there
are here with us, but might as well be
shoeless on the shore of some eastern sea
for all we care.
Well, not we, but you know what I mean.
Some things it's hard to draw a line between.

So now she wants to know what it would cost
to make things right. I tell her, honey, we've tossed
the question back and forth from time to time,
but to make things right, you have to know they're not.

And, anyway,
it doesn't matter if it wouldn't cost a lot—
a boatload of dollars or a dime—
it would still be more than some might want to pay.
Some would say that to say what you're going to give
to help somebody you never heard of live
like you-know-who,
you have to decide what you think somebody is worth,
which hangs on the cost of the bed bloodied at birth.
Child, what I'm telling you is true.

Figured by that, your dog is worth
more—and consequently is better fed—
than half the humans on earth.

Go to bed.

Means to an End

There'll come a day
when you let loose and slip away.
Even when those around you beg you not to,
you've got to.

Such words assume
that you're lying back in a quiet room,
glancing up between a cough and a wince
to count your friends

bent over the bed.
You could, of course, go instead
in a manner that makes the newspaper seem to say
$F = ma$.

Could Be

we'd be better to our kind
and even find
some way we might continue to exist
if we were on the endangered species list.

At Her 1:30 Appt. Mrs. Simmons Tries
to Explain What Happened

When I think of how it used to be,
it doesn't seem like eleven years have passed.
Remember when you thought about Saturday night
in church on Sunday morning? It went that fast—
the afternoon we met, the disheartening distance,
the night I heard him talking in my sleep,
and then the letting in, the folding out,
the coming together both of us knew would keep.

My mother told me nothing could be all good,
or last forever. I didn't argue with her,
even though something inside of me didn't agree.
I rolled on my tongue the rumor that something could.

And it was like milk and flour, him mixing with me,
one common concoction that nothing could ever spoil.

Then someone turned to the wrong recipe—
We read it in the dark, night after night.
Add cold water and slowly bring to a boil.
When the water was gone, something began to burn.
Good? No. Last forever? I'm afraid it might.

At Seventy-Five Suddenly

What do I know that I didn't know at ten?
I'm not sure I know what I knew then,
but I guess there are things I hadn't seen yet
and haven't known long enough to forget—

that everyone wants to be first, moving too fast
to see that we always save the best till last;
that a brain hoping the heart will not outlast it
won't care a whit if the heart lives decades past it;
that while I'm appreciative and almost proud
of the short but widening years I've been allowed,
through all the cherishing I recognize
that each of them contributes to my demise.

What still makes staying a good bit better than going
is stirring awake morning by morning knowing
I wake with a woman who never thought it odd
to think of the universe as the mind of God,
and thought it consoling to think that dead I'd be
wherever it was I was before I was me.

Love, thank you for this, and for something I can't spell out—
that unlettered word our breathing is all about.

Yesterday, Today

I find it sundown disturbing and passing strange
when people say, "God will never change."
Where is the priest or preacher who understands
that God expands when the universe expands?
God, who is love married to mathematics
and speaks to us in the language of quantum mechanics
is all being. All being is God. Still,
where there's a single act of free will
there's something God didn't know was going to be
or the will that brought it about was not free.

So then God knows what God didn't know before.
This is what we call learning, when a mind holds more
on Wednesday than Tuesday. If, as we like to say,
we are what we know, then day to any day
God's not the same. I've thanked God for that on
every church bench and barstool I've sat on.

The Alphabet as Part of What We Are

Some of whom we came from came for a chance.
Others came indentured, others in chains,
to these potential, then united, states,
except for those who crossed the Bering Straits,
but they were immigrants, too, although they came
before there was a colony to name.
We're still astounded to find ourselves here,
children of brave and slave and musketeer,
coolie and buccaneer and wetback,
what we call white and yellow, red and black,
believing in living together and learning to.

Knowing how flesh can fail, minds misconstrue,
we have to wonder how we have come this far
toward what we want to be, being what we are.

Part of what keeps us restless and dreaming ahead
is paper printed with ink, words to be read,
thoughts to be spread about, newspapers and books,
journals and magazines—for lingering looks,
on slow strolls in the garden called the brain,
at long impressions where a truth has lain.

Digital Sex

Well, she was bored, surfing the sites alone.
Well, he was bored in the chat room where he met her.
They clicked on pretty much the same things
and as they got to know each other better

he thought he liked her a lot. So did she.
He was the happiest man in the whole town
until he came to know a little too late
that what she saw and wanted she dragged down.

She thought she'd got herself a hard drive
and a charming ram to boot when he told her, "I'm
at your command, my Eve. I'll eat your apple."
But then he showed her a floppy every time.

Poem without a Title or Closing Line

The alarm sounds at six and he rolls over,
wondering what he can find to rhyme with that.
No. Say that he slips out from under the cover

wide awake when the alarm goes off at six
and showers and shaves in fifteen minutes flat.
Nothing ever goes wrong that he can't fix

with his ear for rhyme and a good sense of rhythm.
He learned this years ago from an old professor
who gave his students something to carry with them.

"Life," he said, "is a poem. An art and a craft.
Do you understand?" The nodding kid said, "Yessir,"
and went to work at once revising his draft.

She said she'd be on the corner at eight or so,
and told him she wouldn't stand there long alone.
He can't tell where the poem's about to go.

She's going to tell him what the doctor said.
She wouldn't tell him on the telephone.
If he could only have it clear in his head

whose feet they followed, where they enjambed that night.
He thinks he remembers he may have had a shot
or two or three more than he normally might.

He shrugged that off until she told him—well—
until she said she might be you-know-what.
If he'd lived his life as a rondeau or villanelle,

he'd know what was ahead, but that was fine.
His pattern allowed surprises, and more fun.
Still he was having trouble finding a line

to spell out the woman she was and, what was worse—
he'd been afraid of this from line one—
everything she did was free verse.

So now he understands what's meant by screwing
up. He feels his iambs going flat
and wonders what he's come to, what he'll be doing

'til resolution undoes all the bother.
And what will he ever find to rhyme with that?

Notes toward a Commencement Address

Some day you might throw a dictionary away
when, just to see spelled out what's pulling you down,
you look up "tired" and find what it says so far off
it's out of town.

The problem will be that you're scuttling ahead of yourself
when a lot of people whose days you're paid to share
believe they've built their homes in days to come
and want you there.

But even behaving toward paychecks, a wedding, a child,
you'll want to spend your days in the present tense—
with occasional nights in the slower, sweet subjunctive,
if that makes sense.

Here's a key to the doors of today. Don't swap
for a pass to a place you'll never see, anyhow.
It hides behind tonight, and when you find it
it's suddenly now.

So when they tell you, "It's all in tomorrow—Come on!"
say to the shaking heads that call you a fool,
"Hey, I'd hold you up. You're moving too fast."
Tell them you're sorry, bow low, and wave with an arm
that might almost be erasing a board in school.

Thinking of Leaving the Church the Young
Preacher Thinks Again

I wanted to find what nobody's ever found,
what all of us want to have and never can,
the answer we've argued about and knelt to and blamed,
the answer we tell ourselves has seen us from somewhere
just out of our sight since human life began—
that fancied answer.

                         You'd think we might by now
have found the hands to shake ourselves free
of tangling hopes at the hint of some Christmas presence—
seeing as how it has nothing to do with what
we pay for our clothes, or the reasons we won't or will
let the dog back in, or whether the coffee's hot.

Ah, but still . . .

Separatio in Loco

He lives all alone now, in the home they bought,
and finally seems to be managing, more or less.
Not the way he was, of course, with her,
who lives alone now, too, at the same address.

The Fourteen-Line Confession of a Retro-Poet

What is it we're doing here? What does it mean
to fashion lines that are units of syntax and sound?
What's the point of a pattern? Has anyone found
the hand of a god in this? Has anyone seen

in all of the counted feet, the foot of One?
Why don't we all just say what we have to say
and stop behaving as if the language were clay
to be shaped into verbal pots, or wool to be spun

to thread, to fabric? Answers squirm about
inside my fountain pen. I'd leave them there
and go on writing lines of certain doubt,
but I know that I've woven something I have to wear.

Why don't we just sling everything on the
        page and let it lie there in whatever
        fashion it falls in without fussing about
        whether you can understand it or
        not and all that prosodic stuff,
        like we were living in the
        world we live in now?
Lord, help us—that's what we'd do if we knew how.

Her Mind Made Up Again to Kill Herself
She Explains It to Herself

It's strange to be the only one who knows
that tomorrow the whole damn show is going to close,
when the tumbling sun
drags behind it the end of everyone
and of everything we've memorized and made—
turtles and television, megabytes and molasses,
bumblebees, bricks and liquor and lemonade,
shoes and toothbrushes, bras, and the common cold,
all about to be turned out of time and space
where no complexion is plain or young or old,
a place where there is no place,
where there is no door, no bed,
and no one to blame,
where nothing is all there can be.
Where has anything been but in my head?

Still, you could say, in a way it's sort of a shame
to leave with nobody about to sit down to dinner
waiting maybe for me.
A shame even not to be there, a glass of wine
lifted to somebody's birthday. Maybe mine.

Thinking about Relativity, Cosmology, and Final Causes
An Ordinary Sunday Afternoon

So say there was a beginning. When, then? And how?
So if there was nothing before there was anything,
where was there nothing? And where is nothing now?

Well, nothing is lying next to what we know,
that being next to nothing. Nevertheless,
we know that questions of matter, of time and space,
are equally answered *no way at all* and *yes.*

While we can barely believe that what is can be,
there never can be nothing—two truths at once
simple and impossible to see.
Hard as it is to conceive of infinity empty,
the world we see and hear, smell, taste, and touch
seems just as unlikely, no matter that we're here,
certain only that we're not certain of much.

I touch and see and hear and taste and smell
the world that seems to be. For all I can tell,
time passes, the sun is a young and mid-size star,
earth and the atom are real, and so are we,
and you still make it matter that we are.

For George Haley, About to Go to the Gambia

on his appointment to the land
from which his ancestors
were shipped in bondage

"I read that a friend of yours is about to be
ambassador to his own," a neighbor said.
"Right," I said, to be sociable. You know me.
What I ought to have said to her instead

is that you're not my friend; you are my brother.
"How so?" she'd say. We'd say we found it so
when each of us came to find himself in the other
and found we knew what those in a family know,

then came to see over the tumbling years
a larger family than family sometimes seems;
to see—far down, where the surface disappears—
that all who carry their mothers' and fathers' dreams,

all those whose dreams are borne by their daughters and sons,
were kin from the first word spoken, and still are.
I want to believe that everyone knew this once.
We came from the same soil. It circles a star.

Some Words on the Wedding of a Good Woman

Think of the several things a circle can mean:
a family, friends, a line without an end
and yet a line completed. We have seen
ourselves going in circles. This is to send

a simple observation about rings
two lovers exchange this ordinary, awesome day.
Scholars tell us that of all the things
we take as symbols—things that somehow say

what words cannot—the circle was the first
in every culture, as even with the wheel,
the circle as machine, humanity burst
out of the shadowy cave and all the while

constructed rites that, circling down the years,
have said to generations who we are,
from those gone before us, to ours, to yours.
No symbol of any kind has come so far

to play a part in what your hearts profess
this day—a sign of sacred things unspoken
as these two rings. Go wear them in happiness.
May all your circles bend but be unbroken.

Time and the Tilting Earth

Back barely half a slow century past
this house was built in a yard a yard or so deep.
Beneath the land was a longtime city dump.
Glass and plastic and metal work their way to the air
and there they tell me things that were long untold
of how we once were, in a world that was.

Here sits someone drinking a Nehi soda,
hearing someone sing on a foot-wide record
wobbling around the pole of a lazy table,
barely a turn a second, one song on a side.

Somebody here bending over the fender
of a car with a running board and no seat belts
gives up on a carburetor and goes into the house
to catch a favorite show on the Philco set.

Here, holding a box the size of an ice bucket,
someone takes a photograph of someone.
Here someone files the colorless picture away
in a wooden box that one day leaves a hinge.

Nobody knows I'm watching. I think Hello,
but even the loudest thought comes back unheard.

Someday, maybe, someone crossing a playground
will touch the toe of a shoe to this fountain pen,
see someone like me writing something,
and wonder a second or two what it might have been.

"Scientists at NASA are trying to create
rudimentary forms of life in a test tube
that will be able to survive, grow, and reproduce
on their own."

—AP news release

How do we know, things being what they are,
with so much we call human going wrong,
that this long leap, so frightening and so far,
was not how somebody planned it all along?

Again on the Date of Her Death
He Remembers the Marriage

He smiles down the gallery of years,
the memory-crowded hallways of his head,
back to the moment they met, the hopeful hello,
his rocking recollection of every bed.

The Greatest among You Shall Be the Least

Beyond science, beyond the arts by far,
forgetting the rabbi, forgetting the preacher and priest,
nothing tells us more about what we are
than getting an envelope back marked *deceased*.

For a Shy Young Woman, a Look at How She Came, Who Tells Me Luck Doesn't Know Her Name

Come contemplate the odds, for a moment or two,
against your becoming the being you're coming to be,
against there ever having been a you
to think of yourself as the only I and me.

Think of the two who would be your father and mother
coming themselves from the same mathematical churn
then living long enough to choose each other,
then coming together—the instant they did—to turn

your first two particles loose in the same place.
Think how many sperm were there, to burst
inside one ovum, when none could form your face
but the waiting egg and the one that got there first.

For eons luck has looked toward where you are.
In every generation, since sex was the key,
a small doorway to you has been left ajar
so one who was no one else could come to be.

Talking about the Retirement of Someone
Not Soon Forgotten

For Richard Wentworth

We've come together here to mark the end
of the luminous, long career of a good friend.
As one of the fortunate who, since books began,
were privileged to be published by this man,
there's much that I want to say, but I'd be remiss
if I left unsaid one thing to say about him—
There's no greener laurel to lay on a leader than this,
that he did it right so we could do it without him.

The Young Preacher Talks to Himself
at the Corner Café

If you can take a moment of my time
I thought we'd have another cup of coffee.
There's something we still haven't talked about.
It won't be easy. Pretend this is a poem.
It's true and it's not true. Just hear me out.

Standing heavy beside a hospital bed
after a school bus wreck with one survivor,
a preacher put his palms together and said,
"God has a purpose for this child."

If we can hear the unsaid side of that,
"God had no use for all the other children,"
then do we understand God from the raw beginning?

I might still have a couple of questions to ask
about where we see ourselves now from the stumbling start,
all of us coming from clay in God's own hands.

What could God say? *Go to hell.* Or maybe,
You still don't get it, do you? Bless your heart.

To Think of Them There

We've always wanted to know the frame we're in,
what there was before we came to be,
if virtue is our invention, what's meant by sin,
if there's a life called immortality
or if we go to chemistry when we're dead.

Well, you'll probably think that I'm a fool
for saying something I think ought to be said.

Our universe could be a molecule
far too small to be seen by the naked eye
of beings we've never imagined, who mix their genes,
work their mathematics, prepare to die,
who have no more need and no more means
to know we're here than to call into question what
they call a world. I simply have to assume
that one of them—some youngster, like as not—
will ask the foolish question in a room
of scholars and scholars-to-be, will say, "Who knows
who or what we are? These molecules
might each be a solar system, systems like those
we think we know". . . ok . . . so we'd have to be fools.
Still, it's something like fun to think of them there,
pouring sex into sex to make babies and drinking air.

Quatrain to an Old Friend

You say you want to discuss the nature of things?
Let's talk about how everything came to be.
Every male mammal has nipples.
Could you please explain that to me?

A Ten-Year-Old in Joint Custody
Writes Her First Poem
When Her Father Gets Married Again

You guess she's going to let me put my head on her pillow?
She will. I know she will. Oh,
yes. Oh, yes!
I know she will. I guess.

He Listens to Himself Talking to Himself

I may have asked you. Forgive me if I forgot.
How did the first of anything come to exist?
It came into being from where, gelled from what?
It may be the What on which most souls insist,
but that couldn't answer the question. How did it start
when there was nothing to start from, when there was no place?
What became the brains that say we're a part
of a population from nonexistent space?

By what jealous arm does gravity pull us down?
How was it to become, when there was no time?
By what heard verb or adjective or noun
did some ear come to recognize a rhyme?

The words How and When are not small.
The answers to them would fill in almost all
the holes in our heads but—standing here—what do we do
with questions like that? I'm going to leave it to you.

About the Physicality of Being

So matter doesn't matter, someone said.

What you say cannot be more important
than the air that carries the words,
and every word is heard
by a complex of shapes.
In how many poems in English
is "word" rhymed with "heard"?

You want to say the answer
would seem absurd.

He Gets Around to Answering the Old Question

He doesn't see as well as he thinks he remembers.
His fingers sometimes find it hard to bend.
He often can't find the name to go with a face.
Sometimes he doesn't hear but decides to pretend.

Weekends, week by week, are closer together.
Sometimes he has to sit down to put on his pants.
No lady seems to mind if he calls her Honey,
never grins nor even throws a glance.

Sometimes he's told himself what all this means.
"Every year some more of me is dead,
but there's a lot of stuff still left to collapse."
He started to laugh but talked to himself instead.

"Think of yourself as a plumbing system, a clock.
As soon as you're done, you start to come undone.
It's almost interesting when you pay attention,
how working parts stop working, one by one.

So now you've asked me the oldest question of all.
You want to know how I'm doing. I told you before,
I'm dying. Been at it for years. Still, I think
I could hang a few more calendars on the door."

A Poem Wants Me

A poem wants me to write it. It rattles my door.
I woke up at three with a sense there was something to say.
I don't know what it wants to be about
or why it came to me to have its way.

Now it rattles a window. I see a hand.
I see a spider web, a torn glove.
I see a single shoe, a dead dog.
I hear a woman talking about love.

It rubs against the glass like a new idea
trying to find a shape, trying to stay.
I still don't know where it came from, how it got here,
or what it wants the shapes of my ink to say.

Ours

Ours is one of countless universes
inside of which none knows how many millions
of galaxies spin, each with uncounted planets,
inviting into our heads unnumbered aliens,

probably something like people, creatures that think,
which leads—as thinking does—to hows and whys,
maybe toward a god we've wanted to know
was up there only for us. A holy surprise.

If we don't slam the door, we have to ask
if every whirling, life-supporting clod
belongs to its own high-watcher of souls to be saved.
We may want to think again of the grandeur of God.

If there is one for all of us, try to imagine
the One turning attention to a prayer
of a woman in Houston fretting about her husband,
where he was last night, who else was there.

Poem to Be Read at My Deathbed

Well, here we are again. Who could have known
I would have been here still to read what you wrote?

We're going to miss you. I can say that for sure.
As surely as you could. Thank you for your note.